COOKING *with* PHEELING

© 2011 KRAFT Foods

All rights reserved.

Published by Kraft Foods. Three Lakes Drive, Northfield, IL 60093

For inquiries regarding this book, contact Kraft Foods Global, Inc.
at 1-800-634-1984

Printed in Italy by NAVA Press

Art direction, design and layout by mcgarrybowen Chicago

PHILADELPHIA, PHILLY and REAL WOMEN OF PHILADELPHIA
are trademarks of Kraft Foods

ISBN 978-0-615-47934-7

COOKING *with* PHEELING

THE NEWEST AND TASTIEST RECIPES AND IDEAS FROM PHILADELPHIA

TABLE *of* CONTENTS

ENRICHING
EXPERIENCES

People have always come together over great food.

With PHILADELPHIA, these gatherings get even richer and more meaningful. There's just something about this cheese that goes beyond how wonderful it tastes. Conversations start up, smiles come out. With dishes and ideas for every occasion, PHILLY makes room for everyone at the table.

ABOUT *this* COOKBOOK

With PHILADELPHIA, the making can be as fun as the eating. Whether you have hours to linger in the kitchen, or need to whip up something in minutes, this cookbook captures it all, from start to delicious finish.

With recipes from three different sources—PHILADELPHIA Classics, REAL WOMEN OF PHILADELPHIA and PHILADELPHIA Cooking Creme—you're sure to find the inspiration for whatever and whomever you're cooking for.

Throughout these pages, we've added tips and dollops of information to make cooking with PHILLY simple and enjoyable. Be sure to add your own twist to recipes and share your results online on the REAL WOMEN OF PHILADELPHIA site. So get started! Great cooking experiences are waiting.

PHILADELPHIA Classics are exactly that: Your go-tos.
Your tried and trues.

The dishes that come through every time. Here you'll rediscover the
magic of PHILLY. How it's the key to that incredible cheesecake. The secret
to that luscious spaghetti sauce. And expect some new surprises too,
because there's really no end to what your PHILLY can do.

REAL WOMEN OF PHILADELPHIA

REAL WOMEN OF PHILADELPHIA
is our online community of PHILLY phanatics.

realwomenofphiladelphia.com

Cooks of all skill levels who share a passion for mixing it up with PHILLY.
Members share their recipes and stories, post videos, as well as participate
in online contests. In this section, you'll discover some of the tasty things
they've come up with: whole new takes on delicious appetizers, entrees,
sides and desserts. With the richness of PHILLY always at the heart of it all.

PHILADELPHIA Cooking Creme has taken PHILLY and creamy to a whole new level.

It's quick and easy to use—just stirring it in can stir up your favorite old recipes. Or if you're looking for some enticing new ones, you'll find them here. Ready to bring the phlavor? Just turn the page.

APPETIZERS

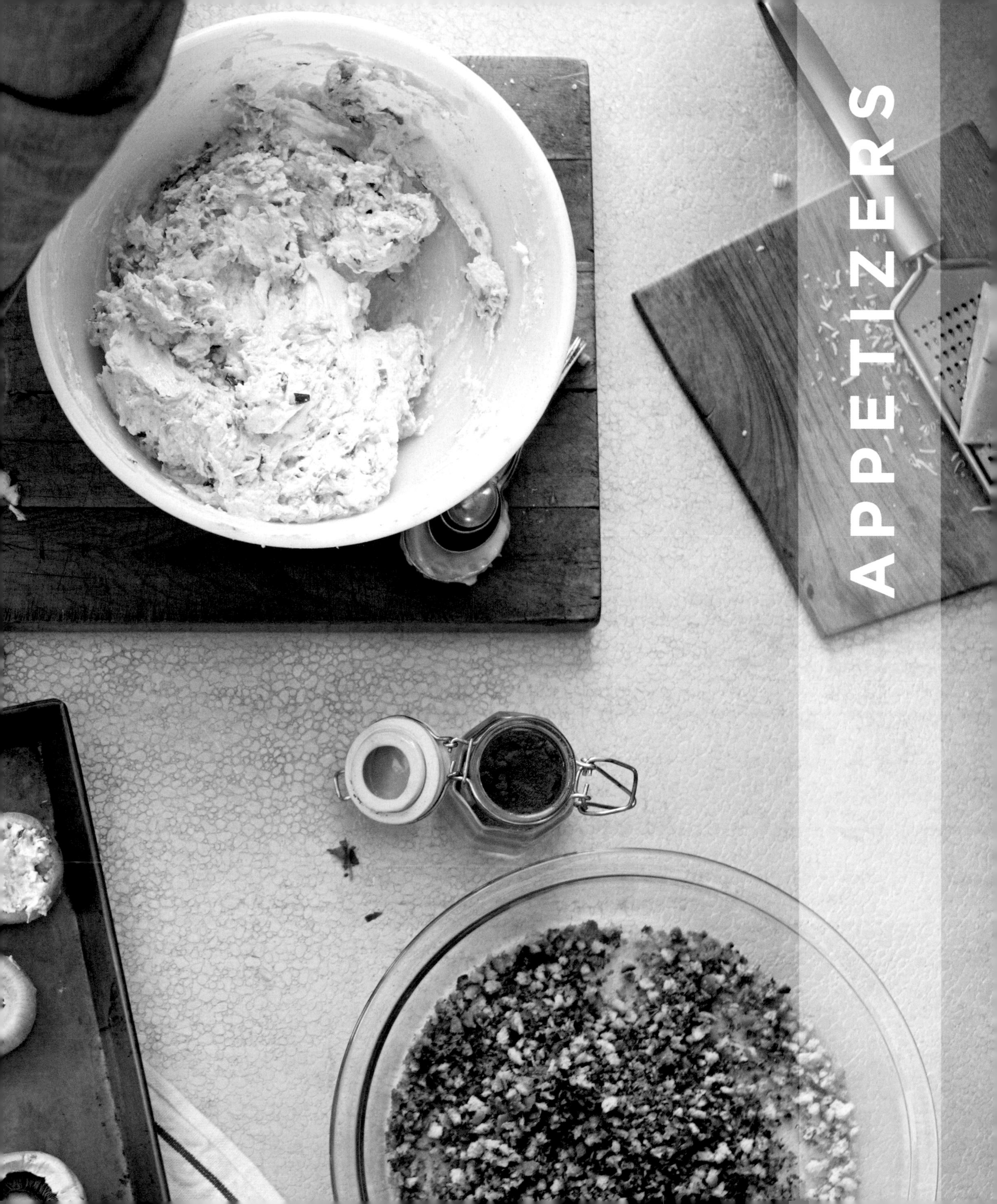

Sassy Tailgate Sandwiches

Prep Time:
35 minutes

Total Time:
1 hour

Makes:
12 servings

1 pkg. (12 count) Hawaiian bread rolls
1 lb. shaved Black Forest ham
12 slices Gruyère cheese
1 tub (8 oz.) PHILADELPHIA Chive & Onion Cream Cheese Spread
½ cup butter, melted
1 Tbsp. Worcestershire sauce
½ Tbsp. dried minced onion
¼ cup grated Parmesan cheese

1 Cut all rolls in half. Place roll bottoms in 9x13-inch pan.

2 Place equal amounts of ham on each roll bottom. Top with Gruyère.

3 On each of the roll tops, spread a generous amount of the cream cheese spread. Return the tops to the bottoms, making sandwiches.

4 In a separate bowl, mix together the butter, Worcestershire sauce, onion and Parmesan cheese. Pour over your sandwiches and let sit for at least 20 minutes. (You can make these ahead of time and allow to sit in fridge overnight.)

5 Place sandwiches, covered in foil, in a preheated 350°F oven. Bake for 20 minutes or until warmed through.

SUBMITTED BY:

REAL WOMEN OF PHILADELPHIA
Season 1 Host
Caryn Ross

Baked Crab Rangoon

Prep Time:
20 minutes

Total Time:
40 minutes

Makes:
12 servings

6 oz. white crabmeat, canned or fresh, drained, flaked

4 oz. (½ of 8-oz. pkg.) PHILADELPHIA Neufchatel Cheese, softened

2 green onions, thinly sliced

¼ cup reduced fat mayonnaise

12 wonton wrappers

1 Heat oven to 350°F.

2 Mix first 4 ingredients.

3 Place 1 wonton wrapper in each of 12 muffin cups sprayed with cooking spray, extending edges of wrappers over sides of cups. Fill with crab mixture.

4 Bake 18 to 20 min. or until edges of cups are golden brown and filling is heated through.

SPECIAL EXTRA:

Garnish with chopped green onions just before serving.

TIP:

For crispier crab rangoon, bake wonton wrappers in muffin cups at 350°F for 5 to 7 min. or until lightly browned. Fill with crabmeat mixture and bake 6 to 8 min. or until filling is heated through.

Warm Reuben Spread

Prep Time:
15 minutes

Total Time:
35 minutes

Makes:
2½ cups spread
or 20 servings,
2 Tbsp. each

 4 oz. (½ of 8-oz. pkg.) PHILADELPHIA Cream Cheese, softened
 ½ cup Thousand Island dressing
 ¼ lb. sliced deli corned beef, chopped (about 1 cup)
 ¾ cup well-drained sauerkraut
 1 pkg. (8 oz.) Swiss cheese slices, chopped

1 Heat oven to 350°F.

2 Mix cream cheese and dressing in medium bowl; stir in all remaining ingredients.

3 Spread onto bottom of 9-inch pie plate or shallow dish.

4 Bake 20 min. or until heated through. Serve warm with rye bread or crackers.

SERVING SUGGESTION:

Serve with dill pickle chips.

TIP:

Instead of baking the prepared spread, microwave it to save time. Assemble dip as directed in shallow microwaveable dish. Microwave on HIGH 2 to 3 min. or until heated through. Serve as directed.

Sweet & Spicy Orange Meatballs

Prep Time:	**Total Time:**	**Makes:**
10 minutes	40 minutes	10 servings

1   pkg. (32 oz.) frozen fully cooked turkey meatballs
1   jar (12 oz.) orange marmalade
¼   cup reduced sodium soy sauce
2   Tbsp. chili-garlic sauce
¾   cup (¾ of 8-oz. tub) PHILADELPHIA Chive & Onion Cream
    Cheese Spread
¼   tsp. ground ginger
2   Tbsp. chopped fresh chives (optional)

1   Place all ingredients except fresh chives in a saucepan; cover
      and bring to a simmer on medium-low heat, stirring occasionally.
      Continue cooking 15 to 20 min. or until heated through.

2   Top with fresh chives, if desired.

SUBMITTED BY:

*REAL WOMEN OF
PHILADELPHIA
Community Member
Mindie Hilton*

TIP:

*Add more chili-garlic sauce
if you like spicier foods.*

Hot Crab and Red Pepper Dip

Prep Time:
10 minutes

Total Time:
30 minutes

Makes:
3 cups spread or
24 servings

1½	cups shredded mozzarella cheese, divided
1	pkg. (8 oz.) PHILADELPHIA Neufchatel Cheese, softened
1	tsp. garlic powder
1	tsp. Italian seasoning
1	red pepper, chopped
1	small onion, finely chopped
6	oz. white crabmeat, canned or fresh, drained

1 Heat oven to 375°F.

2 Reserve ½ cup mozzarella; refrigerate until ready to use. Mix all remaining ingredients until well blended.

3 Spread onto 9-inch pie plate.

4 Bake 20 min. or until crab mixture is heated through and top is lightly browned. Top with reserved mozzarella. Serve with crackers or bread of your choice.

MAKE AHEAD:

Prepare spread as directed, but do not bake. Refrigerate up to 2 days. When ready to serve, bake at 375°F for 25 min. or until heated through. Top with the reserved mozzarella, then serve as directed.

Cheese & Pesto Bread Bake

Prep Time:	**Total Time:**	**Makes:**
10 minutes	40 minutes	12 servings

1 can (4 oz.) reduced fat refrigerated crescent dinner rolls
1 pkg. (8 oz.) PHILADELPHIA Neufchatel Cheese
2 Tbsp. pesto
2 Tbsp. chopped roasted red peppers
1 egg, beaten

1 Heat oven to 350°F.

2 Unroll dough on lightly greased baking sheet; firmly press seams together to form 12x4-inch rectangle.

3 Cut Neufchatel horizontally in half. Place 1 Neufchatel piece on half of dough; top with 1 Tbsp. pesto and peppers. Cover with remaining Neufchatel piece; spread with remaining pesto. Brush dough with egg; fold in half to enclose filling. Press edges of dough together to seal. Brush top with any remaining egg.

4 Bake 15 to 18 min. or until lightly browned. Cool 10 min. Serve with crackers and cut-up fresh vegetables.

MAKE AHEAD:

Assemble recipe on baking sheet as directed. Refrigerate up to 4 hours. When ready to serve, uncover and bake as directed.

Caribbean Nachos

Prep Time:
15 minutes

Total Time:
25 minutes

Makes:
4 servings

4   plantains (yellow with some black), cut diagonally into
    ½-inch-wide slices

½   cup vegetable oil

1   cup peach and mango salsa

3   oz. PHILADELPHIA Cream Cheese

1   Tbsp. hot sauce

2   cups shredded Monterey Jack cheese

1   cup romaine lettuce, shredded

1   cup sour cream

1   large tomato, seeded and diced

1   avocado, cut into small cubes

1 Heat the oil in a large nonstick skillet on medium heat. Add
    plantain slices and fry 2 minutes on each side. Remove to a paper
    towel-lined plate.

2 Lightly flatten the plantains with the bottom of a small glass.
    Heat oil again and fry each slice 2 minutes on each side. Transfer
    to a paper towel-lined plate.

3 Meanwhile, pour the salsa into a small saucepan. Stir in the cream
    cheese and hot sauce. Cook over low heat until the cream cheese
    is melted, stirring frequently.

4 Arrange plantains on a serving plate. Pour the salsa mixture over
    them; sprinkle with the shredded cheese. Top with the lettuce,
    sour cream, tomato and avocado. Serve warm.

SUBMITTED BY:

*REAL WOMEN OF
PHILADELPHIA
Community Member
Pamela Shank*

Polynesian Cheese Round

Prep Time:
20 minutes

Total Time:
1 hour
20 minutes
(incl. refrigerating)

Makes:
15 servings

2   cups macadamia nuts, toasted, chopped and divided

2   tubs (8 oz. each) PHILADELPHIA Cream Cheese Spread

¾   cup finely chopped fresh pineapple, well drained

6   green onions, finely chopped

¼   cup sweetened flaked coconut, toasted

1   tsp. seasoned salt

1   tsp. rum extract

1   Reserve 1 cup nuts. Mix remaining nuts with all remaining ingredients until well blended.

2   Shape into 2-inch-thick round on parchment paper. Top with reserved nuts; press gently into cheese round to secure.

3   Refrigerate 1 hour.

SUBMITTED BY:

REAL WOMEN OF PHILADELPHIA Community Member Jane McMillan

SUBSTITUTE:

Prepare using canned crushed pineapple and/or coconut extract.

Chicken and Sweet Potato Empanadas

Prep Time:
15 minutes

Total Time:
45 minutes

Makes:
8 servings

1   box (14.1 oz.) refrigerated pie crusts
1   medium sweet potato, baked, cooled, peeled
2   tsp. cumin
2   tsp. PICKAPEPPA™ Sauce
1   cup diced cooked chicken
½   cup frozen green peas
4   oz. (½ of 8-oz. pkg.) PHILADELPHIA Cream Cheese, cubed
1   cup salsa
¼   cup diced peaches, fresh or frozen
1   tsp. lime juice

1   Heat oven to 400°F.

2   Remove pie crusts from refrigerator.

3   In a medium bowl, mash potato with cumin and PICKAPEPPA™ sauce. Stir in chicken, peas and cream cheese with fork.

4   Unroll crusts; cut each into 4 wedges. Spread about ¼ cup chicken filling onto each wedge to within ½ inch of both long sides; brush edges of dough with water. Fold each wedge lengthwise in half to enclose filling; press edges together to seal. Place on baking sheet.

5   Bake 30 min. or until golden brown. Cut each empanada into thirds.

6   Combine salsa, peaches and lime juice. Serve with the empanadas.

SUBMITTED BY:

*REAL WOMEN OF
PHILADELPHIA
Community Member
Jackie Brown*

PICKAPEPPA™ Sauce is a product of the Pickapeppa Co. LTD

Savory Three-Cheese Spread

Prep Time:
10 minutes

Total Time:
40 minutes

Makes:
1¼ cups or 10 servings,
2 Tbsp. each

1   pkg. (8 oz.) PHILADELPHIA Cream Cheese, softened
1   cup shredded Cheddar cheese
3   slices smoked ham, finely chopped
¼   cup grated Parmesan cheese
1   Tbsp. chopped red bell peppers
1   Tbsp. sliced green onions
¼   tsp. ground red pepper (cayenne)

1   Heat oven to 350°F.

2   Combine ingredients; spoon into casserole sprayed with cooking spray.

3   Bake 25 to 30 min. or until heated through. Serve with crackers or bread of your choice.

SUBSTITUTE:

Substitute sliced jalapeno peppers or chopped roasted red peppers for the bell peppers and green onions.

PHILLY Stuffed Mushrooms

Prep Time:	**Total Time:**	**Makes:**
20 minutes	50 minutes	10 servings

3 pkg. (8 oz. each) mushrooms

2 pkg. (8 oz. each) PHILADELPHIA Cream Cheese, softened

1 pkt. Italian dressing mix

¼ cup mayonnaise

2 Tbsp. minced onion

1 Tbsp. chopped fresh parsley

1 cup grated Parmesan cheese

⅛ tsp. ground red pepper (cayenne)

1 pkg. stuffing mix

3 Tbsp. butter, melted

1 Heat oven to 350°F.

2 Clean mushrooms and remove stems; set aside.

3 Mix cream cheese, Italian dressing mix, mayonnaise, onion, parsley, Parmesan cheese and red pepper; set aside.

4 Put stuffing mix in separate bowl. Stuff mushrooms with the cream cheese mixture.

5 Press cream cheese side of mushrooms into the stuffing mix until well coated.

6 Place mushrooms, cream cheese sides up, on a baking pan, then drizzle with the melted butter.

7 Bake for 30 min.

SUBMITTED BY:

*REAL WOMEN OF
PHILADELPHIA
Season 1 Finalist
Annette Gladys*

SIDES

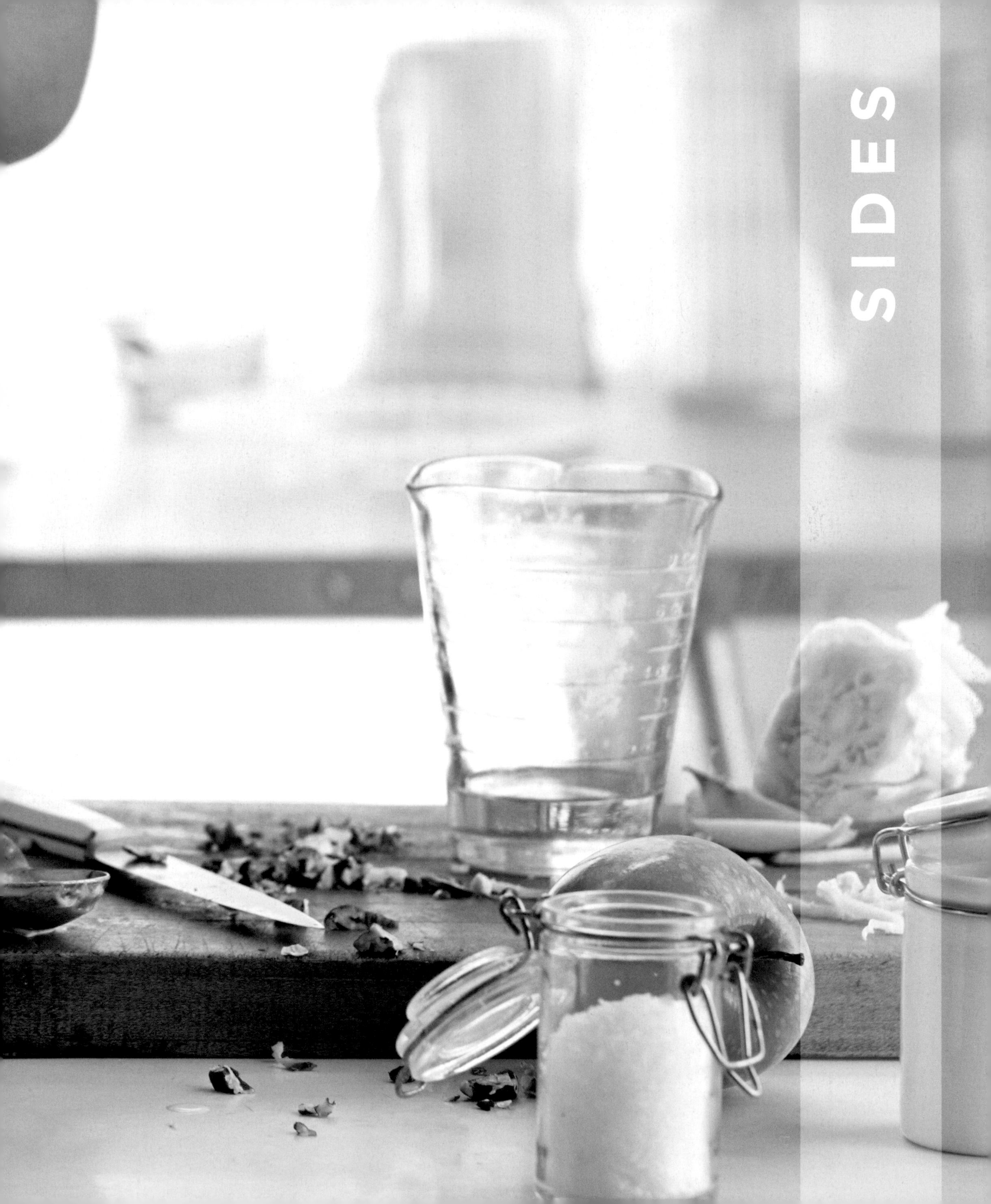

Asparagus & Parmesan Cream Pastry

Prep Time:
15 minutes

Total Time:
37 minutes

Makes:
8 servings

1   sheet frozen puff pastry dough
1   lb. fresh asparagus spears (16 spears)
1   pkg. (8 oz.) PHILADELPHIA Cream Cheese, softened
½   cup grated Parmesan cheese
5   fresh basil leaves, chopped
3   Tbsp. fresh lemon juice
1   pinch sea salt
2   Tbsp. olive oil
2   Tbsp. shaved Parmesan cheese

1   Heat oven to 400°F.

2   Remove pastry dough from freezer; thaw 10 min. Meanwhile, wash asparagus; trim so it is 1½ inches shorter than width of pastry sheet.

3   In a medium bowl, combine cream cheese, grated Parmesan, basil and lemon juice.

4   Unfold dough onto baking sheet sprayed with cooking spray. Cut into 4 rectangles; separate slightly. Spread with cream cheese mixture almost to edges of dough. Press 4 asparagus spears into cream cheese mixture on each rectangle, alternating directions of tips. Sprinkle with salt; drizzle with oil.

5   Bake 18 to 22 min. or until golden brown. Cut in half.

6   Place on platter. Garnish with shaved Parmesan cheese.

SUBMITTED BY:

REAL WOMEN OF PHILADELPHIA
Season 1 Host
Mandy Heaston

Creamy Vegetable Orzo

Prep Time:	**Total Time:**	**Makes:**
10 minutes	35 minutes	6 servings, about ½ cup each

1	Tbsp. oil
1	small onion, chopped
½	cup each chopped green and red peppers
1	cup frozen corn
¾	cup orzo pasta, uncooked
1	can (14½ oz.) fat free, reduced sodium chicken broth
½	cup (½ of 8-oz. tub) PHILADELPHIA Chive & Onion ⅓ Less Fat Cream Cheese

1 Heat oil in large skillet on medium heat. Add onions; cook 4 min., stirring frequently. Stir in peppers and corn; cook and stir 2 min. Add orzo; cook and stir 1 min.

2 Stir in broth; bring to boil on high heat. Simmer on medium-low heat 10 to 12 min. or until orzo and vegetables are tender and most of the liquid is absorbed, stirring occasionally.

3 Add reduced fat cream cheese; cook 1 to 2 min. or until cream cheese is melted and sauce is well blended, stirring constantly.

SPECIAL EXTRA:

Add 1 Tbsp. chopped fresh herbs, such as basil or rosemary, to the cooked vegetables with the broth.

Baked Cauliflower and Bacon au Gratin

Prep Time:
10 minutes

Total Time:
25 minutes

Makes:
6 servings

1   large head of cauliflower
2   Tbsp. butter
5   large baby bella mushrooms, sliced
1   shallot, minced
½   leek, white and light green parts, diced
1   Tbsp. flour
4   oz. (½ of 8-oz. pkg.) PHILADELPHIA Cream Cheese,
      cubed and softened
¼   cup white wine
     salt and black pepper to taste
4   slices bacon
2   cups shredded Cheddar cheese

1   Bring large pot of salted water to boil. Add cauliflower; cover. Cook 10 to 12 min. or until tender. Drain.

2   Melt butter in large skillet on medium heat. Add mushrooms and shallots; cook and stir 5 min. Stir in leeks; cook and stir 3 min. Add flour and cream cheese; cook and stir until cream cheese is melted and mixture is well blended. Stir in wine. Season with salt and pepper; simmer for a few minutes.

3   In a separate skillet, cook bacon until crisp; drain on paper towels. Chop into small pieces.

4   Place cauliflower in large baking dish. Add cream cheese mixture; stir to combine. Top with bacon and shredded cheese.

5   Heat broiler. Broil cauliflower mixture 5 min. or until golden brown.

SUBMITTED BY:

REAL WOMEN OF PHILADELPHIA Community Member Terri Luciana

SERVING SUGGESTION:

Prepare as directed, spooning cauliflower mixture evenly into 6 (8-oz.) buttered ramekins. Top with bacon and cheese. Broil as directed.

Mediterranean Baked Spinach

Prep Time:
10 minutes

Total Time:
1 hour

Makes:
10 servings,
½ cup each

1 lb. fresh baby spinach leaves

6 cups boiling water

4 eggs

¾ cup milk

4 oz. (½ of 8-oz. pkg.) PHILADELPHIA Cream Cheese, softened

1 cup crumbled feta cheese with basil & tomato, divided

1 Heat oven to 350°F.

2 Place spinach in colander in sink. Pour boiling water over spinach; cool.

3 Meanwhile, beat eggs and milk with whisk in large bowl until well blended. Add cream cheese; mix well. Stir in ½ cup feta. Squeeze excess moisture from spinach; stir into cream cheese mixture. Spread into a 2-qt. baking dish; top with remaining feta. Cover.

4 Bake 50 min. or until center is set, uncovering after 30 min.

SHORTCUT:

Substitute 2 pkg. (10 oz. each) frozen spinach, thawed and squeezed dry, for the cooled blanched fresh spinach.

SPECIAL EXTRA:

For added flavor and crunch, sprinkle with ¼ cup toasted pine nuts before serving.

Santa Fe Chicken Enchilada Soup

Prep Time:
10 minutes

Total Time:
28 minutes

Makes:
6 servings,
about 1 cup each

4   corn tortillas (6 inch), cut into strips
1   tsp. oil
1   lb. boneless, skinless chicken breasts, cut into bite-size pieces
1   tub (10 oz.) PHILADELPHIA Santa Fe Blend Cooking Creme
1   cup milk
1   can (15 oz.) black beans, rinsed
1   can (11 oz.) corn with red and green bell peppers, drained
1   can (14.5 oz.) diced tomatoes, drained
¼   cup chopped fresh cilantro

1   Heat oven to 400°F.

2   Toss tortilla strips with oil; spread into single layer on baking sheet. Bake 10 to 12 min. or until crisp, stirring occasionally.

3   Meanwhile, cook chicken in large nonstick saucepan sprayed with cooking spray on medium-high heat 8 to 10 min. or until chicken is done, stirring frequently. Stir in Cooking Creme, milk, beans, corn and tomatoes; simmer on medium-low heat 6 to 8 min. or until heated through, stirring frequently.

4   Serve soup topped with tortilla strips and cilantro.

SPECIAL EXTRA:
Serve with lime wedges to give the soup a little citrus kick.

Bacon & Maple Scalloped Potatoes

Prep Time:
15 minutes

Total Time:
1 hour
30 minutes

Makes:
8 servings,
about 1 cup each

1	red onion, thinly sliced
4	oz. (½ of 8-oz. pkg.) PHILADELPHIA Cream Cheese, cubed
1¼	cups fat free, reduced sodium chicken broth
½	cup milk
3	slices pre-cooked bacon, chopped
¼	cup maple-flavored or pancake syrup
2	lb. Yukon gold potatoes (about 6), cut into ¼-inch-thick slices
1	cup KRAFT Shredded Triple Cheddar Cheese with a Touch of PHILADELPHIA

1 Heat oven to 400°F.

2 Cook onions in large skillet sprayed with cooking spray on medium-high heat 3 to 5 min. or until crisp-tender, stirring frequently. Remove onions from skillet.

3 Add cream cheese, broth and milk to skillet; cook and stir on medium-low heat 5 min. or until cream cheese is melted and mixture is well blended. Remove from heat; stir in bacon and syrup.

4 Place half the potatoes in 13x9-inch baking dish sprayed with cooking spray; cover with layers of onions and shredded cheese. Top with remaining potatoes and cream cheese sauce; cover.

5 Bake 1 hour 5 min. or until potatoes are tender and top is golden brown, uncovering after 50 min.

SUBSTITUTE:

Create two-tone scalloped potatoes by substituting sweet potatoes for half the Yukon gold potatoes.

Twice-Baked Sweet Potatoes

Prep Time:	**Total Time:**	**Makes:**
10 minutes	53 minutes	4 servings

2   large sweet potatoes (1½ lb.)

2   oz. (¼ of 8-oz. pkg.) PHILADELPHIA Neufchatel Cheese, cubed

2   Tbsp. fat free milk

1   Tbsp. brown sugar

¼   tsp. ground cinnamon

¼   cup chopped pecans

1   Heat oven to 425°F.

2   Cut potatoes lengthwise in half; place, cut side down, in foil-lined 15x10x1-inch pan. Bake 30 to 35 min. or until tender.

3   Scoop out centers of potatoes into bowl, leaving ¼-inch-thick shells. Add Neufchatel, milk, sugar and cinnamon to potato flesh; mash until well blended.

4   Fill shells with potato mixture; top with nuts. Bake 8 min. or until potatoes are heated through and nuts are toasted.

SHORTCUT:

Pierce whole sweet potatoes with fork; wrap in damp paper towels. Microwave on HIGH 7 to 8 min. or until tender. Cut potatoes in half; scoop out centers and continue as directed.

Swiss Chard au Gratin

Prep Time:	**Total Time:**	**Makes:**
10 minutes	58 minutes	6 servings

6   strips bacon

6   Tbsp. butter

2   cloves garlic, minced

2   shallots, finely chopped

4   oz. (½ of 8-oz. pkg.) PHILADELPHIA Cream Cheese

4   oz. Havarti cheese

1½ cups heavy cream

     dash salt and pepper

4   Tbsp. olive oil

4   lb. green Swiss chard

1   cup Panko bread crumbs

1   Heat oven to 350°F.

2   Cook bacon in a medium skillet over moderately high heat until the fat is rendered, 3 to 5 min. Transfer bacon to paper towels, keeping the drippings in the skillet. Add the butter along with the garlic and ½ of the shallots to skillet. Cook over moderate heat until softened, about 2 min. Add cream cheese and Havarti, and whisk in heavy cream. Simmer until reduced by half, about 8 min. Season with salt and pepper.

3   Heat a large skillet over moderate heat. Add olive oil and saute Swiss chard leaves with the remaining shallots until softened, about 3 min. Season with salt and pepper. Transfer chard leaves to a shallow baking dish and cover with the cream cheese mixture. Top with Panko and crumbled bacon. Bake until crumbs are toasted and the casserole is bubbling, about 30 min.

SUBMITTED BY:

REAL WOMEN OF PHILADELPHIA
Season 1 Finalist
Jacqui Nicholson

Poblano Pepper Popper

Prep Time:
10 minutes

Total Time:
20 minutes

Makes:
4 servings

2 large poblano peppers
1 pkg. (8 oz.) PHILADELPHIA Cream Cheese, softened
1 Tbsp. diced jalapeno peppers, divided
   salt and black pepper
¾ cup cornmeal
⅓ cup canned creamed corn
3 Tbsp. milk
2 Tbsp. oil
1 egg
1½ cups shredded Cheddar cheese, divided

1 Roast poblano peppers until they are charred but still hold their shape. Cool; remove charred skins. Cut poblanos in half; remove seeds.

2 Mix cream cheese, half of the jalapenos and a dash each of the salt and black pepper until blended.

3 Place poblanos, cut sides up, on a baking pan. Spoon cream cheese mixture evenly into peppers.

4 Mix cornmeal, corn, milk, oil, egg, remaining jalapenos, half the Cheddar cheese and a dash each of salt and black pepper.

5 Spoon over cream cheese mixture in poblanos.

6 Bake at 350°F for 20 min. Top with the remaining Cheddar cheese; bake an additional 10 min. or until cheese is melted.

SUBMITTED BY:

REAL WOMEN OF PHILADELPHIA Community Member Dee Guelcher

Lean Green Slaw

Prep Time:	**Total Time:**	**Makes:**
10 minutes	20 minutes	4 servings

5   cups shredded Napa cabbage

1   Granny Smith apple, cut into 8 wedges, then cut crosswise into
¼-inch-thick slices

½   cup (½ of 8-oz. tub) PHILADELPHIA Honey Nut Flavor Cream
Cheese Spread

¼   cup mayonnaise

2   Tbsp. seasoned rice vinegar

1   Combine cabbage and apples in a 1½-qt. serving bowl.

2   In a small mixing bowl, whisk together cream cheese spread,
mayonnaise and vinegar until blended. Add to cabbage mixture;
mix well.

3   Serve immediately, or cover and refrigerate until ready to serve.

SUBMITTED BY:

*REAL WOMEN OF
PHILADELPHIA
Community Member
Laurie L. Figone*

SPECIAL EXTRA:

*Sprinkle with 2 Tbsp.
chopped pecans for
added crunch.*

Sautéed Onion and Corn Casserole

Prep Time:
15 minutes

Total Time:
55 minutes

Makes:
8 servings

½ cup finely diced onions

1 cup finely chopped mushrooms

4 Tbsp. butter, divided

¼ cup flour

1 can (14 oz.) cream-style corn

1 can (14 oz.) whole kernel corn, drained

½ cup (½ of 8-oz. tub) PHILADELPHIA Chive & Onion Cream Cheese Spread

½ cup shredded Gruyère cheese

½ tsp. salt

¼ tsp. white pepper

¼ cup crushed butter crackers

1 Heat oven to 350°F. Sauté onions and mushrooms in 2 Tbsp. butter in a medium skillet until tender and lightly browned.

2 Sprinkle with flour; cook and stir 1 min.

3 Stir in the cream of corn; cook 1 min.

4 Remove from heat. Stir in all remaining ingredients except for the cracker crumbs and remaining butter.

5 Spoon into a casserole dish or oven-proof skillet sprayed with cooking spray.

6 Top with crackers. Melt remaining 2 Tbsp. butter; drizzle over cracker crumbs.

7 Bake 35 to 40 min. or until bubbly and golden brown.

SUBMITTED BY:

REAL WOMEN OF PHILADELPHIA Community Member Lee Bailey

Chicken Joy Bundles and Rice

Prep Time:
20 minutes

Total Time:
52 minutes

Makes:
4 servings,
2 bundles each

4	boneless, skinless chicken breasts, cut crosswise in half
	pinch salt and pepper
1	pkg. (8 oz.) PHILADELPHIA Cream Cheese, softened
½	cup chopped spring onions
1	tsp. finely chopped fresh tarragon
8	strips turkey bacon
4	Tbsp. butter, divided
2¼	cups chicken broth
2	cups uncooked rice pilaf (10-min. variety)
3	cloves garlic, chopped
4	Tbsp. fresh lemon juice
2	tsp. lemon zest
3	Tbsp. chopped fresh dill
1	Tbsp. chopped fresh parsley

1 Heat oven to 375°F.

2 Season chicken with salt and pepper.

3 Mix cream cheese, onions and tarragon; spread onto chicken. Roll up, starting at one short end of each piece. Wrap with bacon.

4 Place chicken in ungreased baking dish. Melt 1 Tbsp. butter; brush onto chicken. Cover.

5 Bake 20 to 25 min. or until chicken is done. Meanwhile, bring chicken broth, rice and garlic to boil in saucepan. Reduce heat and simmer 10 min. or until liquid is absorbed.

6 Transfer chicken to broiler. Broil 5 to 7 min. or until golden brown.

7 Remove rice from heat. Stir in remaining butter, lemon juice, zest and dill; spoon onto platter. Top with chicken. Ladle pan juices over chicken; sprinkle with parsley.

SUBMITTED BY:

REAL WOMEN OF PHILADELPHIA
Season 1 Host
Sheila Cutchlow

Tomato-Basil Pizza

Prep Time:
10 minutes

Total Time:
22 minutes

Makes:
6 servings

1 ready-to-use baked pizza crust (12 inch)
½ cup PHILADELPHIA Italian Cheese and Herb Cooking Creme
1 tomato, thinly sliced
½ cup shredded mozzarella cheese
8 fresh basil leaves, torn

1 Heat oven to 425°F.

2 Spread pizza crust with Cooking Creme; top with tomatoes and cheese.

3 Place crust directly on middle oven rack.

4 Bake 10 to 12 min. or until cheese is melted. Sprinkle with basil.

SUBSTITUTE:

Substitute drained roasted red pepper slices for the tomatoes.

Zesty Zucchini & Spinach Rigatoni

Prep Time:
20 minutes

Total Time:
45 minutes

Makes:
6 servings,
1⅓ cups each

8	oz. (½ of 16-oz. pkg.) rigatoni pasta, uncooked
1	tsp. oil
1	zucchini, sliced
½	lb. sliced fresh mushrooms
2	cloves garlic, minced
1	Tbsp. flour
½	tsp. each dried basil leaves, oregano leaves and crushed red pepper
1	cup fat free, reduced sodium chicken broth
4	oz. (½ of 8-oz. pkg.) PHILADELPHIA Neufchatel Cheese, cubed
1	pkg. (6 oz.) baby spinach leaves
¼	cup grated Parmesan cheese
1½	cups KRAFT Shredded Mozzarella Cheese with a Touch of PHILADELPHIA, divided

1 Heat oven to 375°F.

2 Cook pasta in large saucepan as directed on package, omitting salt.

3 Meanwhile, heat oil in large skillet on medium heat. Add zucchini, mushrooms and garlic; cook and stir 3 to 4 min. or until zucchini is crisp-tender. Add flour and seasonings; cook and stir 1 min. Stir in broth; cook and stir 2 to 3 min. or until thickened. Add Neufchatel; cook and stir 2 to 3 min. or until melted.

4 Drain pasta; return to pan. Add zucchini mixture, spinach, Parmesan and ½ cup mozzarella; mix lightly. Spoon into 2-qt. casserole sprayed with cooking spray; top with remaining mozzarella.

5 Bake 10 min. or until mozzarella is melted.

TIP:

To prepare perfect pasta, follow package directions to ensure enough water is used. Add pasta to boiling water and cook until al dente (tender but still a little firm to the bite). To prevent pasta from sticking, add slowly to boiling water and stir frequently. Adding oil to the cooking water is not recommended as some sauces may not cling to pasta coated with oil.

Salmon en Papillote

Prep Time:
20 minutes

Total Time:
35 minutes

Makes:
4 servings

4   oz. (½ of 8-oz. tub) PHILADELPHIA Chive & Onion
    Cream Cheese Spread

2   Tbsp. extra virgin olive oil

2   Tbsp. chopped sun-dried tomatoes

4   boneless, skinless salmon fillets (4 or 5 oz. each)

¼   cup good-quality white wine

2   garlic cloves, minced

½   tsp. ground sea salt

¼   tsp. ground black pepper

½   small sweet onion, thinly sliced

12 stalks thin asparagus, trimmed, cut in half

½   tsp. lemon zest

1 Heat oven to 400°F.

2 Mix cream cheese spread, oil and tomatoes. Cut slit in one side of each salmon fillet to form pouch; fill with cream cheese mixture.

3 Fold each of 4 (15x12-inch) sheets of parchment paper crosswise in half; cut into half-heart shape, using the fold as the straight edge. Open each heart; spray with cooking spray.

4 Mix wine, garlic, salt and pepper. Place salmon fillet on half of each heart; top with onions, asparagus, wine mixture and zest.

5 Fold top half of each heart over salmon to completely cover it. Starting at top of heart, fold about ¼ inch of the edge toward center, and then fold again to make tight seal. Continue "rolling the hem" around edge of parchment, pinching each roll tightly to seal. When the "hem" reaches the bottom of the heart tip, twist about 1 inch of the bottom tightly to seal. Place packets on large baking sheet.

6 Bake 15 min. Place each packet on a plate. Use a sharp knife to cut a large "X" in top of each packet. Peel back parchment with tongs.

SUBMITTED BY:

REAL WOMEN OF PHILADELPHIA Community Member Betsy Chan

TIP:

Salmon is cooked if it flakes easily with a fork. If salmon is not cooked, return salmon to the oven (keeping the parchment peeled back). Bake an additional 1 to 3 min. or until salmon is done.

Hearty Ham & Cheese Pot Pie

Prep Time:
15 minutes

Total Time:
47 minutes

Makes:
4 servings

1   ham steak (6 oz.), chopped
1   cup shredded Cheddar cheese
1   cup frozen broccoli cuts, thawed, drained
1   cup frozen cauliflower florets, thawed, drained
2   green onions, chopped
½   cup (½ of 8-oz. tub) PHILADELPHIA Chive & Onion
        ⅓ Less Fat Cream Cheese
1   ready-to-use refrigerated pie crust (½ of 14.1-oz. pkg.)
1   egg
1   Tbsp. water

1   Heat oven to 400°F.

2   Combine first 5 ingredients. Microwave cream cheese spread in microwaveable bowl on HIGH 1 min. or until completely melted, stirring every 15 sec. Add to ham mixture; mix well. Spoon into 4 (6-oz.) ramekins.

3   Unroll pie crust on lightly floured surface; roll to 12-inch circle. Cut into 4 circles with 5-inch round cookie cutter; discard remaining trimmings.

4   Beat egg and water until well blended; brush onto top edges of ramekins. Top with pie crust circles; press gently onto top edges of ramekins to seal. Brush lightly with egg wash. Discard any remaining egg wash. Place ramekins on baking sheet. Cut slits in crusts to vent.

5   Bake 30 to 32 min. or until golden brown.

TIP:

If you don't have a 5-inch cookie cutter, invert a 5-inch-diameter bowl or clean can onto pastry; trace around edge with small, sharp knife. Repeat to cut out the remaining 3 circles.

Baked Penne with Beef

Prep Time:
15 minutes

Total Time:
47 minutes

Makes:
4 servings

½ lb. extra-lean ground beef

½ cup each chopped onions and green peppers

1 jar (24 oz.) spaghetti sauce

1 tub (10 oz.) PHILADELPHIA Italian Cheese and Herb
   Cooking Creme, divided

1 cup shredded mozzarella cheese, divided

3 cups cooked penne pasta

1 Heat oven to 350°F.

2 Brown meat with vegetables in large nonstick skillet. Stir in
spaghetti sauce, ¾ cup Cooking Creme and ½ cup mozzarella;
cook and stir 2 to 3 min. or until mozzarella is melted. Add
pasta; mix lightly.

3 Spoon into 2-qt. casserole; top with remaining Cooking Creme
and mozzarella. Cover.

4 Bake 20 min. or until heated through, uncovering after 15 min.

SUBSTITUTE:

*Substitute Italian sausage
for the ground beef.*

Roast Pork Tenderloin Supper

Prep Time:
20 minutes

Total Time:
45 minutes

Makes:
4 servings

2   pork tenderloins (1½ lb.)
¼   cup Dijon mustard
2   tsp. dried thyme leaves
1   pkg. (6 oz.) stuffing mix for chicken
½   cup fat free, reduced sodium chicken broth
4   oz. (½ of 8-oz. pkg.) PHILADELPHIA Neufchatel Cheese, cubed
1   lb. fresh green beans, trimmed, steamed

1   Heat oven to 400°F.

2   Heat large nonstick skillet on medium heat. Add meat; cook 5 min. or until browned on all sides, turning occasionally. Remove meat from skillet, reserving meat drippings in skillet; place meat in 13x9-inch baking dish. Mix mustard and thyme; spread onto meat.

3   Bake 20 to 25 min. or until meat is done (160°F). Transfer to carving board; tent with foil. Let stand 5 min. Meanwhile, prepare stuffing as directed on package, reducing the butter or margarine to 1 Tbsp.

4   Add broth to same skillet. Bring to boil on high heat. Reduce heat to medium-low. Add Neufchatel; cook 2 min. or until Neufchatel is completely melted and mixture is well blended, stirring constantly.

5   Cut meat into thin slices. Serve topped with the Neufchatel sauce along with the stuffing and beans.

TIP:

If you purchased the broth in a 32-oz. pkg., store remaining broth in refrigerator up to 1 week. Or if you purchased a 14-oz. can, pour the remaining broth into a glass container; store in refrigerator up to 1 week.

Chicken, Broccoli and Red Pepper Rotini

Prep Time:
10 minutes

Total Time:
22 minutes

Makes:
4 servings,
1½ cups each

2 tsp. oil

1 lb. boneless, skinless chicken breast halves, cut into bite-size pieces

2 cups broccoli florets

1 red pepper, cut into short, thin strips

1 tub (10 oz.) PHILADELPHIA Savory Garlic Cooking Creme

2 cups hot, cooked rotini pasta

2 Tbsp. grated Parmesan cheese

1 Heat oil in large skillet on medium heat. Add chicken and vegetables; cook and stir 7 to 8 min. or until chicken is done and vegetables are crisp-tender.

2 Add Cooking Creme; cook 2 to 3 min. or until heated through, stirring frequently.

3 Stir in pasta. Sprinkle with Parmesan.

SUBSTITUTE:

Substitute 1 lb. uncooked, deveined, peeled medium shrimp for the chicken. Cook and stir peppers and broccoli in hot oil in large skillet 5 min. Add shrimp; cook and stir 3 to 4 min. or until shrimp turn pink. Add Cooking Creme; continue as directed.

Tuscan Tilapia

Prep Time:
5 minutes

Total Time:
17 minutes

Makes:
4 servings

1   Tbsp. oil
4   tilapia fillets (1 lb.)
¼   tsp. black pepper
1   tub (10 oz.) PHILADELPHIA Tomato & Basil Cooking Creme
1   cup frozen peas
2   cups hot, cooked long-grain white rice

1   Heat oil in large nonstick skillet on medium heat. Add fish; sprinkle with pepper. Cook 3 min. on each side or until fish is browned on both sides and flakes easily with fork. Remove from skillet; cover to keep warm.

2   Add Cooking Creme to skillet; cook and stir 2 min. Remove ¼ cup Cooking Creme; set aside. Add peas and rice to remaining Cooking Creme in skillet; cook and stir 3 min. or until heated through.

3   Spoon rice mixture onto platter; top with fish and reserved sauce.

SUBSTITUTE:

Substitute 4 small boneless, skinless chicken breast halves (1 lb.) for the fish. Cook 5 to 6 min. on each side or until done (165°F), then continue as directed.

SPECIAL EXTRA:

Sprinkle with diced fresh tomatoes before serving.

Homestyle Chicken Pot Pie

Prep Time:
10 minutes

Total Time:
48 minutes

Makes:
6 servings

1   lb. boneless, skinless chicken breasts, cut into bite-size pieces
2   cups frozen mixed vegetables (carrots, corn, green beans, peas), thawed, drained
1   tub (10 oz.) PHILADELPHIA Savory Garlic Cooking Creme
1   ready-to-use refrigerated pie crust (½ of 14.1-oz. pkg.)

1   Heat oven to 400°F.

2   Cook and stir chicken in large nonstick skillet on medium heat 5 to 6 min. or until chicken is lightly browned. Add vegetables; cook 1 to 2 min. or until heated through. Stir in Cooking Creme; spoon into 9-inch pie plate.

3   Cover with crust; seal and flute edge. Cut several slits in crust. Place pie plate on baking sheet.

4   Bake 25 to 30 min. or until golden brown.

SHORTCUT:

Prepare using a rotisserie chicken purchased from your supermarket. Remove chicken from the bones, then chop or shred it for use in preparing this recipe. Combine 3 cups chopped cooked chicken, vegetables and Cooking Creme; spoon into pie plate. Continue as directed.

White Chicken Chili

Prep Time:
10 minutes

Total Time:
27 minutes

Makes:
4 servings,
1 cup each

1	large onion, chopped
1	lb. boneless, skinless chicken breasts, cut into strips
½	tsp. each ground cumin and dried oregano leaves
1	tub (10 oz.) PHILADELPHIA Savory Garlic Cooking Creme
½	cup milk
1	can (15 oz.) white beans, rinsed
1	can (4 oz.) green chiles, undrained
½	cup Mexican-style finely shredded four-cheese blend
½	cup chopped tomatoes
2	Tbsp. chopped fresh cilantro
½	avocado, chopped

1 Cook onions in large saucepan sprayed with cooking spray on medium heat 4 to 5 min. or until crisp-tender, stirring frequently. Add chicken, cumin and oregano; cook and stir 6 to 7 min. or until chicken is done.

2 Stir in next 4 ingredients; simmer on medium-low heat 5 min. or until heated through, stirring occasionally.

3 Serve topped with remaining ingredients.

SERVING SUGGESTION:

Serve over hot cooked rice.

TIP:

For thicker consistency, prepare chili as directed. Remove about ½ cup beans; mash with fork. Return to chili; stir. Serve as directed.

Sautéed Scallops in Ginger-Garlic Sauce

Prep Time:
15 minutes

Total Time:
45 minutes

Makes:
6 servings

2	Tbsp. garlic-flavored or regular olive oil
1½	lb. sea scallops, cut in half
2	cups fresh broccoli florets
½	cup coconut milk
¾	cup low sodium chicken broth
¼	cup minced ginger root
4	cloves garlic, minced
1	tsp. fish sauce (nam pla)
4	oz. (½ of 8-oz. pkg.) PHILADELPHIA Cream Cheese, cubed
	salt and pepper
3	cups hot cooked tagliatelle pasta

1 Heat olive oil in a 12-inch nonstick skillet over medium heat. Add scallops; sauté just until opaque. (Do not overcook.) Remove from skillet; cover to keep warm.

2 To blanch broccoli, add it to a saucepan of lightly salted boiling water. Cook 1 or 2 min. or just until broccoli turns bright green. Remove with slotted spoon, then immediately place in large bowl of cold water to stop the cooking process; drain.

3 In large skillet, combine coconut milk, chicken broth, ginger, garlic and fish sauce. Bring to simmer. Add cream cheese; cook until cream cheese is melted and sauce is well blended. Season with salt and pepper to taste.

4 Add pasta, broccoli and scallops to sauce in skillet; mix lightly.

5 Transfer to serving dish. Garnish with chopped green onions and red pepper flakes, if desired.

SUBMITTED BY:

REAL WOMEN OF PHILADELPHIA Community Member Carol A. White

Asparagus, Potato and PHILLY Pizza

Prep Time:
15 minutes

Total Time:
50 minutes

Makes:
6 servings

1 can (13.8 oz.) refrigerated pizza dough

1 clove garlic, minced

1 Tbsp. olive oil

4 green onions, thinly sliced, divided

¾ cup KRAFT Shredded Mozzarella Cheese with a Touch of PHILADELPHIA

¼ lb. fresh asparagus spears, trimmed, cut lengthwise in half, then crosswise into 3-inch lengths

¼ lb. new potatoes, cooked, cooled and thinly sliced

2 Tbsp. shredded Parmesan cheese

3 oz. PHILADELPHIA Cream Cheese, broken into small pieces

1 Heat oven to 450°F.

2 Press pizza dough onto bottom of 15x10x2-inch pan sprayed with cooking spray.

3 Mix garlic and oil; spread half onto crust. Top with half the onions and mozzarella. Toss asparagus with remaining garlic oil; spread over pizza. Top with potatoes, Parmesan and cream cheese.

4 Bake 18 to 20 min. or until crust is golden brown. Sprinkle with remaining onions.

SUBSTITUTE:

Try our recipe for Perfect Parmesan Pizza Dough at kraftrecipes.com. Use ¼ of the recipe to make the crust for this pizza. Reserve remaining dough for later use.

Tex-Mex Beef & Rice Casserole

Prep Time:
20 minutes

Total Time:
50 minutes

Makes:
8 servings,
about 1⅔ cups

1   lb. extra-lean ground beef

1   can (14 oz.) fire-roasted diced tomatoes, undrained

1   can (11 oz.) corn with red and green bell peppers, undrained

½   cup chopped onions

1   tub (10 oz.) PHILADELPHIA Santa Fe Blend Cooking Creme, divided

3   cups cooked long-grain white rice

1   cup shredded Colby & Monterey Jack cheeses, divided

1   cup crushed tortilla chips

3   Tbsp. chopped fresh cilantro

1   Heat oven to 350°F.

2   Brown meat in large nonstick skillet; drain. Return to skillet. Add tomatoes, corn, onions and ¾ cup Cooking Creme; mix well.

3   Combine rice and ½ cup shredded cheese in 13x9-inch baking dish sprayed with cooking spray; spread to cover bottom of dish. Top with layers of meat mixture, remaining Cooking Creme and remaining shredded cheese; cover.

4   Bake 30 min. or until heated through. Top with crushed chips and cilantro.

SERVING SUGGESTION:

Serve over fresh salad greens.

SUBSTITUTE:

Substitute 1 jar (14 oz.) of your favorite salsa for the fire-roasted tomatoes.

91

Chicken with Creamy Roasted Poblanos

Prep Time:
10 minutes

Total Time:
33 minutes

Makes:
6 servings

1 fryer chicken (3 lb.), cut up
1 tub (10 oz.) PHILADELPHIA Original Cooking Creme
2 Tbsp. milk
4 large poblano chiles (1 lb.), roasted, peeled, seeded and cut into strips
4 slices baked ham, chopped
1 tomato, seeded, chopped

1 Cook chicken in large skillet on medium heat 10 min. or until browned on both sides, turning occasionally. Cover; cook 10 min. or until done (165°F.) Drain any liquid from skillet.

2 Stir in Cooking Creme, milk, chiles and ham; cook, covered, on medium-low heat 2 to 3 min. or until heated through, stirring occasionally.

3 Top with tomatoes just before serving.

SPECIAL EXTRA:

To roast poblano chiles, arrange whole chiles on a baking sheet. Broil, 2 to 4 inches from heat, until chiles are completely blackened, turning occasionally. Place in paper bag; close bag. Let stand 20 min. or until chiles are completely cooled. Remove chiles from bag. Using a small knife, peel away blackened skins; discard. Cut chiles in half lengthwise; remove and discard seeds.

Fiesta Shrimp Tacos

Prep Time:
15 minutes

Total Time:
27 minutes

Makes:
4 servings

2   tsp. oil
1   cup thinly sliced onions
1   lb. uncooked, deveined, peeled small shrimp
1   tub (10 oz.) PHILADELPHIA Santa Fe Blend Cooking Creme
8   corn tortillas (6 inch)
1   cup Mexican-style finely shredded four-cheese blend
½   cup shredded purple cabbage
¼   cup sliced radishes
2   Tbsp. chopped fresh cilantro
    juice from 1 lime

1 Heat oil in large nonstick skillet on medium-high heat. Add onions; cook and stir 5 min. Stir in shrimp; cook 3 to 4 min. or until shrimp turn pink, stirring frequently.

2 Add Cooking Creme; cook and stir 2 min.

3 Spoon onto tortillas; top with remaining ingredients.

SUBSTITUTE:

Substitute 3 cups chopped or shredded cooked chicken for the shrimp, cooking until heated through before adding the Cooking Creme.

Lemongrass-Speared Pork Kebabs

Prep Time:
12 minutes

Total Time:
22 minutes

Makes:
4 servings

1   lb. ground pork

6   oz. (¾ of 8-oz. pkg.) PHILADELPHIA Cream Cheese, softened, divided

4   Tbsp. of hoisin sauce, divided

8   stalks lemongrass

2   tsp. of chopped fresh cilantro

1   Heat broiler. Mix the pork, 4 oz. cream cheese and 3 Tbsp. hoisin sauce until well blended. Divide into 8 portions, about ¼ cup each. Shape each into patty; place a lemongrass stalk on center of each patty. Roll the pork mixture around each stem to enclose it. Roll patties to form kebabs.

2   Cover a baking sheet with foil; spray with cooking spray. Place pork kebabs on baking sheet. Broil 5 min. on each side or until meat is golden brown and done.

3   Meanwhile, mix remaining 2 oz. cream cheese and 1 Tbsp. hoisin in microwaveable dish. Microwave on HIGH for 30 sec. or until heated through. Stir in cilantro. Drizzle over kebabs.

SUBMITTED BY:

REAL WOMEN OF PHILADELPHIA Community Member Maria Holguin

SERVING SUGGESTION:

Serve on a bed of hot cooked couscous mixed with a few ground strands of saffron, salt, pepper and a dab of butter.

Georgia Sunshine Fried Chicken

Prep Time:
10 minutes

Total Time:
30 minutes

Makes:
6 servings

1   cup + 2 Tbsp. honey, divided

1   egg, beaten

1½ tsp. minced garlic

¾   cup Georgia pecans, shelled, chopped

¾   cup Panko bread crumbs

    salt

6   boneless, skinless chicken breasts (4 oz. each)

1   cup butter

½   cup orange juice

4   oz. (½ of 8-oz. pkg.) PHILADELPHIA Cream Cheese, cubed

1   Heat oven to 400°F. Cover baking sheet with foil.

2   In a shallow dish, mix 2 Tbsp. honey, egg and garlic. In another shallow dish, combine pecans, bread crumbs and a little salt.

3   Sprinkle chicken breasts with a little salt. Dip in the egg mixture, then immediately roll in the nut mixture. Press crumbs into chicken to secure.

4   Place on baking sheet; sprinkle with any remaining nut mixture.

5   Bake 20 minutes or until golden brown.

6   While chicken bakes, melt butter in skillet over low heat. Stir in remaining 1 cup honey, orange juice and cream cheese; cook and stir until cream cheese is melted and sauce is well blended. Pour sauce over chicken.

SUBMITTED BY:

REAL WOMEN OF PHILADELPHIA Community Member Debi Wood

SERVING SUGGESTION:

Pair with your favorite green vegetable or a spinach leaf salad.

Country Frittata

Prep Time:	**Total Time:**	**Makes:**
10 minutes	28 minutes	6 servings

1   tub (10 oz.) PHILADELPHIA Original Cooking Creme, divided

6   eggs

¼   tsp. black pepper

2   Tbsp. butter

1   cup chopped green peppers

4   green onions, sliced

¼   cup chopped smoked ham

½   cup shredded sharp Cheddar cheese

1   Reserve ¼ cup Cooking Creme. Whisk remaining Cooking Creme with eggs and black pepper until well blended.

2   Melt butter in 10-inch ovenproof skillet on medium heat. Add green peppers; cook and stir 5 min. or until crisp-tender. Stir in egg mixture, onions and ham; cover. Cook on medium-low heat 8 to 9 min. or until center is almost set.

3   Heat broiler. Uncover frittata; sprinkle with Cheddar. Broil, 6 inches from heat, 2 to 3 min. or center is set and Cheddar is melted. Drizzle with reserved Cooking Creme.

SUBSTITUTE:

Prepare as directed, substituting chopped pepperoni for the ham and shredded mozzarella cheese for the Cheddar.

Teriyaki Salmon with Tasty Vegetable Rice

Prep Time:
15 minutes

Total Time:
30 minutes

Makes:
4 servings

1   Tbsp. oil
¼   cup teriyaki sauce, divided
1   clove garlic, minced
4   salmon fillets (1 lb.)
¾   cup pea pods, halved
¾   cup shredded carrots
1   tub (10 oz.) PHILADELPHIA Original Cooking Creme
2   cups hot, cooked long-grain white rice
2   green onions, sliced

1   Heat oil in large nonstick skillet on medium-high heat. Add 1 Tbsp. teriyaki sauce, garlic and fish; cook fish 2 to 3 min. on each side or until fish flakes easily with fork. Remove fish from skillet; cover to keep warm.

2   Add pea pods and carrots to skillet; cook and stir 2 min. or until crisp-tender. Stir in Cooking Creme and remaining teriyaki sauce; cook and stir 2 min. Remove ¼ cup sauce. Stir rice into remaining sauce in skillet.

3   Spoon rice mixture onto platter; top with fish, remaining sauce and onions.

SPECIAL EXTRA:

Garnish with 2 Tbsp. toasted sesame seeds.

Creamy Bacon Fettuccine

Prep Time:
20 minutes

Total Time:
38 minutes

Makes:
4 servings,
1¼ cups each

6   slices bacon, cut into ½-inch pieces

½   cup chopped red onions

1   tub (10 oz.) PHILADELPHIA Italian Cheese and Herb Cooking Creme

½   cup milk

1   cup frozen peas

½   lb. fettuccine, cooked

1   Cook bacon in large skillet until crisp. Remove bacon from skillet with slotted spoon, reserving 2 Tbsp. drippings in skillet. Drain bacon on paper towels.

2   Stir onions into drippings; cook and stir 3 min. or until crisp-tender. Add Cooking Creme, milk and peas; cook and stir 3 min.

3   Add bacon and pasta; stir to coat.

SUBSTITUTE:

Substitute 1 cup chopped smoked ham for the bacon.

Delicious Bacon-Wrapped Pork Loin

Prep Time:
15 minutes

Total Time:
50 minutes

Makes:
6 servings

½ cup peach preserves

1 (or more if desired) canned chipotle peppers in adobo sauce, finely diced

1 large garlic clove, crushed

1 pork tenderloin

8 oz. pork chorizo sausage

1 tub (8 oz.) PHILADELPHIA Garden Vegetable Cream Cheese Spread

3 oz. Mexican-style finely shredded four-cheese blend

1 lb. sliced bacon, divided

⅓ cup brown sugar

dash ground black pepper

1 Heat oven to 400°F.

2 Mix first 3 ingredients until well blended.

3 Open tenderloin on work surface; pound to even thickness. Spread cut side with chorizo, then cream cheese spread; sprinkle with shredded cheese. Roll up tenderloin, starting at one long side.

4 Wrap tenderloin with bacon until completely covered; secure with wooden toothpicks, if needed. Place in cast iron, or heavy-bottom skillet; cook until evenly browned, turning occasionally. Transfer to foil-lined baking dish.

5 Bake 25 min. or until tenderloin reaches 160°F, brushing with preserves mixture for the last 10 min. Transfer to cutting board; let rest 5 to 10 min. before slicing.

6 Meanwhile, chop remaining bacon; cook in same skillet until crisp. Discard all but 1 to 2 tablespoons drippings from skillet. Stir sugar and pepper into bacon and drippings in skillet; cook on low heat until bubbly. Remove from heat.

7 Slice tenderloin; place on platter. Top with bacon.

SUBMITTED BY:

REAL WOMEN OF PHILADELPHIA Season 1 Finalist Suzanne Clark

SERVING SUGGESTION:

Serve with roasted root vegetables.

Creamy Chicken, Bacon & Tomato Pasta

Prep Time:
20 minutes

Total Time:
20 minutes

Makes:
4 servings,
1¾ cups each

3   cups whole wheat farfalle (bow tie pasta), uncooked
1   lb. boneless, skinless chicken breasts, cut into bite-size pieces
3   slices bacon, cooked, crumbled
1   can (14½ oz.) Italian-style diced tomatoes, undrained
4   oz. (½ of 8-oz. pkg.) PHILADELPHIA Neufchatel Cheese, cubed
½   cup water
¼   tsp. pepper
3   Tbsp. grated Parmesan cheese

1   Cook pasta as directed on package.

2   Meanwhile, cook chicken in large skillet on medium heat 5 to 6 min. or until done, stirring occasionally. Add next 5 ingredients; mix well. Cook 3 min. or until Neufchatel is completely melted and mixture is well blended, stirring frequently.

3   Drain pasta; place in large bowl. Add sauce; mix lightly. Sprinkle with Parmesan.

SPECIAL EXTRA:

Sprinkle with chopped fresh Italian parsley before serving.

Sausage & Vegetable Calzones

Prep Time:
10 minutes

Total Time:
35 minutes

Makes:
6 servings

½ lb. bulk Italian sausage

½ lb. sliced fresh mushrooms

1 large red pepper, cut into strips, halved

1 tub (10 oz.) PHILADELPHIA Savory Garlic Cooking Creme

1 cup shredded mozzarella cheese

1 can (10 oz.) refrigerated pizza crust

1 Heat oven to 400°F.

2 Brown sausage with mushrooms and peppers in large nonstick skillet on medium-high heat. Drain; return to skillet. Stir in Cooking Creme and mozzarella. Remove from heat.

3 Unroll pizza dough on clean work surface. Pat out to 15x11-inch rectangle; cut lengthwise in half, then cut each piece crosswise into thirds. Top dough rectangles with sausage mixture; fold in half. Seal edges with fork. Place on baking sheet sprayed with cooking spray.

4 Bake 15 min. or until golden brown.

SPECIAL EXTRA:

Sprinkle each calzone lightly with grated Parmesan cheese before baking.

SUBSTITUTE:

Omit mushrooms. Brown sausage with peppers; drain and return to skillet. Add 1 pkg. (6 oz.) fresh baby spinach; cover and cook 5 to 6 min. or until spinach is wilted. Add Cooking Creme and mozzarella; mix well. Continue as directed.

Easy Chicken Enchiladas

Prep Time:
15 minutes

Total Time:
35 minutes

Makes:
4 servings

1   small onion, chopped

2   tsp. oil

3   cups shredded cooked chicken breasts

1   can (14.5 oz.) no-salt-added diced tomatoes, drained

1   tub (10 oz.) PHILADELPHIA Santa Fe Blend Cooking Creme, divided

½   cup Mexican-style finely shredded four-cheese blend

8   flour tortillas (6 inch)

1   Heat oven to 350°F.

2   Cook and stir onions in hot oil in large skillet on medium heat 4 to 5 min. or until crisp-tender. Stir in chicken, tomatoes, ¾ cup Cooking Creme and shredded cheese.

3   Spoon about ⅓ cup chicken mixture down center of each tortilla; roll up. Place in 13x9-inch baking dish sprayed with cooking spray; top with remaining Cooking Creme. Cover.

4   Bake 15 to 20 min. or until heated through.

SPECIAL EXTRA:

Sprinkle with chopped tomatoes and sliced green onions before serving.

TIP:

To shred chicken, place cooked chicken on cutting board. Use 2 forks or your fingers to pull meat lengthwise in opposite directions, separating it into long shreds.

Chocolate-Topped Linzer Cookies

Prep Time:
45 minutes

Total Time:
2 hours
17 minutes
(incl. refrigerating)

Makes:
2 dozen or 24 servings,
1 cookie each

2¼ cups flour
⅛ tsp. each ground cinnamon, ground cloves and ground nutmeg
1 cup butter, softened
2 cups plus 1 Tbsp. powdered sugar, divided
2 egg yolks
1 cup slivered almonds, finely ground
¾ cup seedless raspberry jam
2 squares semisweet chocolate
4 oz. (½ of 8-oz. pkg.) PHILADELPHIA Cream Cheese, softened

1 Mix flour and spices. Beat butter and 1 cup sugar in large bowl with mixer until well blended. Add egg yolks; mix well. Gradually beat in flour mixture and nuts. Divide dough in half. Shape each half into ball; flatten slightly. Wrap in plastic wrap. Refrigerate 1 hour.

2 Heat oven to 350°F. Roll out each piece of dough on lightly floured surface to ⅛-inch thickness; cut into 24 circles with 2½-inch round cutter, rerolling scraps as necessary. (You will have 48 circles.) Transfer to baking sheets. Use 1-inch round cutter to cut out centers from 24 circles; discard removed centers.

3 Bake 10 to 12 min. or until edges are golden brown. Cool on baking sheets 3 min. Remove to wire racks; cool completely.

4 Spread jam over whole cookies. Use fine-mesh strainer to sprinkle 1 Tbsp. sugar over remaining cut-out cookies; place over jam-topped cookies.

5 Melt chocolate as directed on package. Beat cream cheese with mixer until creamy. Beat in chocolate, then remaining sugar until light and fluffy. Spoon heaping teaspoon chocolate mixture onto center of each cookie; let stand 10 min. or until firm.

TIP:

To grind almonds, use pulsing action to process almonds in food processor until finely ground.

Uptown Lime Tarts with Raspberries

Prep Time:
20 minutes

Total Time:
30 minutes

Makes:
30 servings

2 pkg. (1.9 oz. each) frozen miniature phyllo tart shells

4 oz. (½ of 8-oz. pkg.) PHILADELPHIA Cream Cheese, softened

1 jar (10 oz.) lime curd

1 tub (8 oz.) frozen whipped topping, thawed

⅔ cup raspberry jam

1 Bake tart shells according to package directions; cool completely on a wire rack.

2 Combine the cream cheese, lime curd and whipped topping until well blended. Spoon 1 tsp. jam into each tart shell. Pipe or spoon cream cheese mixture over jam.

3 Garnish with fresh raspberries if desired.

SUBMITTED BY:

REAL WOMEN OF PHILADELPHIA Community Member Pamela Burton

SPECIAL EXTRA:

Dust with powdered sugar just before serving.

Blackberry Cream Cheese Doughnuts

Prep Time:
20 minutes

Total Time:
45 minutes

Makes:
8 servings

3   Tbsp. unsalted butter, melted, divided

1   lb. frozen bread dough, thawed

½   cup (½ of 8-oz. tub) PHILADELPHIA Original Whipped Cream
     Cheese Spread

⅓   cup seedless blackberry jam, warmed

1   Tbsp. milk, heated

½   tsp. vanilla

¾   cup powdered sugar

1   Grease an 11x7-inch baking dish with 1 tsp. butter; set aside.

2   Divide dough into 8 balls. Use rolling pin to roll out each ball on
       lightly floured surface to 5x4-inch rectangle.

3   Spread cream cheese onto each rectangle to within a ½ inch
       of edges; spread jam over cream cheese. Roll up each rectangle
       from one long side to form log; press edges together to seal.
       Bring ends of each log together to form circle; press ends
       together to seal.

4   Place in single layer in prepared baking dish. Brush tops with
       1 Tbsp. of the remaining butter. Cover with clean kitchen towel;
       put in a warm place. Let rise 45 min. or until dough doubles
       in volume.

5   Heat oven to 350°F. Bake doughnuts 20 to 25 min. or until
       golden brown.

6   Brush with 2 tsp. of the remaining butter. Cool for 20 min.

7   Meanwhile, stir milk, remaining 1 Tbsp. butter and vanilla in a
       medium bowl until well blended. Add powdered sugar; whisk
       until smooth. Drizzle over warm doughnuts. Serve warm.

SUBMITTED BY:

*REAL WOMEN OF
PHILADELPHIA
Community Member
Mary Shivers*

Vanilla Mousse Cheesecake

Prep Time:
20 minutes

Total Time:
6 hours
15 minutes
(incl. refrigerating)

Makes:
16 servings

---

4   vanilla wafer cookies, crushed (about 1½ cups)

3   Tbsp. butter or margarine, melted

4   pkg. (8 oz. each) PHILADELPHIA Cream Cheese, softened, divided

1   cup sugar, divided

1   Tbsp. plus 1 tsp. vanilla, divided

3   eggs

1   tub (8 oz.) frozen whipped topping, thawed

---

1   Heat oven to 325°F.

2   Mix wafer crumbs and butter; press onto bottom of 9-inch springform pan.

3   Beat 3 pkg. cream cheese, ¾ cup sugar and 1 Tbsp. vanilla with mixer until well blended. Add eggs, one at a time, mixing on low speed after each just until blended. Pour over crust.

4   Bake 50 to 55 min. or until center is almost set. Run knife around rim of pan to loosen cake; cool completely in pan.

5   Beat remaining cream cheese, sugar and vanilla with mixer in large bowl until well blended. Whisk in whipped topping; spread over cheesecake. Refrigerate 4 hours. Remove rim of pan before serving cheesecake.

SPECIAL EXTRA:

Garnish with fresh berries just before serving.

TIP:

Use bottom of a dry measuring cup to press crumb mixture into bottom of pan.

Rustic Chocolate Bread Pudding

Prep Time:
15 minutes

Total Time:
50 minutes

Makes:
8 servings

½ cup (½ of 8-oz. tub) PHILADELPHIA ⅓ Less Fat Cream Cheese

½ cup packed brown sugar

2 egg whites

½ tsp. ground cinnamon

1¾ cups fat free milk

6 cups cubed whole wheat bread (6 to 8 slices)

2 squares semisweet chocolate, coarsely chopped

1 Heat oven to 350°F.

2 Beat reduced fat cream cheese and sugar in large bowl with mixer until well blended. Add egg whites and cinnamon; mix well. Gradually beat in milk until well blended.

3 Place bread in 8-inch square baking dish; top with chocolate and cream cheese mixture.

4 Bake 30 to 35 min. or until center is set. Cool slightly.

SERVING SUGGESTION:

Spoon into small dishes to serve.

SPECIAL EXTRA:

Top dessert with ½ cup thawed, light whipped topping just before serving.

Cappuccino Cake

Prep Time:
20 minutes

Total Time:
25 minutes

Makes:
10 servings

1   box angel food cake mix
¾   cup double-strength brewed coffee, cooled
1   pkg. (8 oz.) semisweet chocolate, divided
1   pkg. (8 oz.) PHILADELPHIA Cream Cheese, softened
1   cup powdered sugar
2   cups thawed frozen whipped topping

1   Prepare cake as directed on package. Cool completely.

2   Place cake on large plate with rim. Cut 1-inch-thick slice off top of cake; tear top into small pieces. Use to fill center opening of cake.

3   Use skewer to poke holes in top surface of cake; pour coffee evenly over cake, allowing the coffee to soak in. Place in refrigerator until ready to use.

4   Grate about ½ oz. of the chocolate for garnish; set aside. Microwave remaining chocolate in microwaveable bowl on HIGH 1½ min. or until melted, stirring after 1 min.; cool slightly.

5   Beat cream cheese and powdered sugar in medium bowl with mixer until well blended. Add melted chocolate; beat until light and fluffy.

6   Transfer cake to serving dish; frost top with chocolate mixture. Cover with whipped topping. Sprinkle with grated chocolate. Refrigerate until ready to serve.

SUBMITTED BY:

REAL WOMEN OF PHILADELPHIA Community Member Lacey Long

SHORTCUT:

Prepare as directed using a large (10-inch) store-bought angel food cake.

Creamy Lemon Bars

Prep Time:
25 minutes

Total Time:
3 hours
23 minutes
(incl. refrigerating)

Makes:
16 servings

20 reduced fat vanilla wafer cookies, finely crushed (about ¾ cup)

½ cup flour

¼ cup packed brown sugar

¼ cup cold margarine

1 pkg. (8 oz.) PHILADELPHIA Neufchatel Cheese, softened

1 cup granulated sugar

2 eggs

2 Tbsp. flour

3 Tbsp. lemon zest, divided

¼ cup fresh lemon juice

¼ tsp. baking powder

2 tsp. powdered sugar

1 Heat oven to 350°F.

2 Line 8-inch square pan with foil. Mix wafer crumbs, ½ cup flour and brown sugar in medium bowl. Cut in margarine with pastry blender or 2 knives until mixture resembles coarse crumbs; press onto bottom of prepared pan. Bake 15 min.

3 Beat Neufchatel and granulated sugar with mixer until well blended. Add eggs and 2 Tbsp. flour; mix well. Blend in 1 Tbsp. zest, juice and baking powder; pour over crust.

4 Bake 25 to 28 min. or until center is set. Cool completely. Refrigerate 2 hours. Sprinkle with powdered sugar and remaining zest before serving.

SUBSTITUTE:

Substitute 1 Tbsp. each lemon, lime and orange zest for the 3 Tbsp. lemon zest.

TIP:

You should get about 1 Tbsp. zest and 2 Tbsp. juice from 1 lemon.

Layered White Chocolate Crepe Cake

Prep Time:
15 minutes

Total Time:
15 minutes

Makes:
8 servings

1 pkg. (8 oz.) PHILADELPHIA Cream Cheese, softened
4 oz. white chocolate, melted
2 cups whipping cream
7 prepackaged crepes (9 inch)
   cherry topping

1 Beat cream cheese and chocolate in large bowl until well blended. Gradually beat in cream.

2 Spread cream cheese mixture onto 6 crepes; stack on plate. Cover with remaining crepe.

3 Top with cherry topping just before serving.

CHERRY TOPPING:

Heat oven to 400°F. Spoon ¾ lb. pitted fresh cherries into 8-inch square baking dish. Squeeze juice from ½ lemon; mix with 2 Tbsp. honey and a few fresh rosemary sprigs. Drizzle over cherries. Bake 10 min.

SUBMITTED BY:

REAL WOMEN OF PHILADELPHIA Community Member Edwina Gadsby

SPECIAL EXTRA:

Shave an additional white chocolate square into curls. Use to garnish dessert just before serving.

Spiced Pumpkin Cheesecake

Prep Time:
15 minutes

Total Time:
5 hours
45 minutes
(incl. refrigerating)

Makes:
16 servings

---

38 gingersnaps, finely crushed (about 1½ cups)

¼ cup finely chopped pecans

¼ cup butter or margarine, melted

4 pkg. (8 oz. each) PHILADELPHIA Cream Cheese, softened

1 cup sugar

1 can (15 oz.) pumpkin

1 Tbsp. pumpkin pie spice

1 tsp. vanilla

4 eggs

1 Heat oven to 325°F.

2 Mix crumbs, pecans and butter; press onto bottom and 1 inch up side of 9-inch springform pan.

3 Beat cream cheese and sugar in large bowl with mixer until well blended. Add pumpkin, spice and vanilla; mix well. Add eggs, one at a time, mixing on low speed after each just until blended. Pour into crust.

4 Bake 1 hour 20 min. to 1 hour 30 min. or until center is almost set. Loosen cake from rim of pan; cool before removing rim. Refrigerate 4 hours.

SPECIAL EXTRA:

Dust with ground cinnamon or nutmeg before serving.

TIP:

To soften cream cheese, place completely unwrapped package of cream cheese in microwaveable bowl. Microwave on HIGH 10 sec. or just until softened. Add 15 sec. for each additional package of cream cheese.

Mounds of Joy Whipped Pie

Prep Time:
20 minutes

Total Time:
50 minutes
(incl. refrigerating)

Makes:
6 servings

1   pkg. (8 oz.) PHILADELPHIA Cream Cheese, softened
1   cup cream of coconut
1   pkg. (3.9 oz.) cheesecake flavor instant pudding
14   oz. frozen sweetened flaked coconut, divide in ½ and toast ½
2   tubs (8 oz. each) whipped topping, divided
1   OREO pie crust
    hard-shell chocolate ice cream topping (optional)
6   mini chocolate-coated coconut and almond candy bars

1   Blend together softened cream cheese and cream of coconut until smooth and creamy. Add dry pudding mix and beat until well blended.

2   Add ½ thawed, but cold, coconut. Mix well. Fold in 1 tub whipped topping.

3   Pour ½ of pudding mixture into the pie crust. Drizzle with hard-shell chocolate ice cream topping, if desired. Pour second half of pudding mixture over pie.

4   Mix ¾ cup of toasted coconut with remaining tub of whipped topping and spread or pipe on pie.

5   Finish pie by garnishing with mini chocolate-coated coconut and almond candy bars. Sprinkle remaining toasted coconut on pie.

6   Place in freezer 30 minutes or refrigerate for 45 minutes to set. Slice and enjoy!

SUBMITTED BY:

*REAL WOMEN OF PHILADELPHIA
Season 1 Finalist
Debbie Fabre*

TIPS:

Toast coconut on plate in microwave until evenly browned. Stir often to prevent burning. Watch closely. If you wish to use the coconut without toasting, that is also acceptable.

Banana S'Mores

Prep Time:
15 minutes

Total Time:
23 minutes

Makes:
12 servings

3　medium bananas
1　tub (8 oz.) PHILADELPHIA Original Whipped Cream Cheese Spread
1　cup powdered sugar
12　graham crackers, broken in half (24 squares)
3　milk chocolate bars (1.55 oz. each), quartered

1　Split bananas lengthwise and crosswise in half. Heat nonstick skillet sprayed with cooking spray on medium heat. Add bananas; cook 3 to 4 min. or until lightly browned, turning once.

2　In a medium mixing bowl, beat the cream cheese and powdered sugar until creamy.

3　Cover 12 graham cracker squares with chocolate and bananas. Spread remaining graham cracker squares with cream cheese mixture; place, cream cheese side down, on topped graham cracker squares to make s'mores.

SUBMITTED BY:
REAL WOMEN OF PHILADELPHIA Community Member Dawn Hopkinson

French Apple Cake

Prep Time:
15 minutes

Total Time:
50 minutes

Makes:
8 servings

1½ cups granulated sugar, divided

4 tsp. water

½ lemon

6 apples

3 eggs

1 cup flour

8 oz. (2 sticks) butter, softened

4 oz. (½ of 8-oz. pkg.) PHILADELPHIA Cream Cheese, softened

1 tub (8 oz.) PHILADELPHIA Honey Nut Flavor Cream Cheese Spread

1 cup whipping cream

¼ cup powdered sugar

1 Heat oven to 350°F.

2 To prepare the caramel, heat ¾ cup granulated sugar with 4 tsp. water. When the sugar becomes light brown, add the juice of ½ lemon and remove from heat.

3 Coat the bottom and sides of a springform pan with the caramel.

4 Peel, core and thinly slice the apples and arrange in an attractive circular overlapping pattern on the caramel.

5 In a large mixing bowl, beat the eggs with remaining ¾ cup granulated sugar. Add the flour, butter and 4 oz. cream cheese, and continue beating until you have a creamy batter.

6 Pour over apples and caramel and bake for 35 minutes. Let cool slightly prior to turning over onto a decorative cake plate.

WHIPPED TOPPING

While cake is baking, beat cream cheese spread until fluffy. Separately, beat whipping cream until fluffy and then add ¼ cup powdered sugar. Gently fold the beaten cream cheese spread into the whipped cream and chill well, using the freezer if necessary. Top the warm cake slices with a spoonful of the whipped cream mixture and enjoy!

SUBMITTED BY:

REAL WOMEN OF PHILADELPHIA
Season 1 Host
KC Quaretti-Lee

Double Lemon-Poppy Seed Cupcakes

Prep Time:
20 minutes

Total Time:
1 hour
10 minutes
(incl. cooling)

Makes:
30 servings

1	pkg. (2-layer size) lemon cake mix
1	pkg. (3 oz.) lemon flavor gelatin
1¼	cups water
½	cup oil
4	eggs
¼	cup plus ½ tsp. poppy seeds, divided
1	pkg. (8 oz.) PHILADELPHIA Cream Cheese, softened
¼	cup butter, softened
2	Tbsp. fresh lemon juice
1	pkg. (16 oz.) powdered sugar, sifted

1 Heat oven to 350°F.

2 Beat first 5 ingredients with mixer until well blended. Stir in ¼ cup poppy seeds. Spoon into 30 paper-lined muffin cups.

3 Bake 18 to 20 min. or until toothpick inserted in centers comes out clean. Cool in pans 10 min.; remove to wire racks. Cool completely.

4 Beat cream cheese, butter and lemon juice with mixer until well blended. Gradually beat in sugar; spread onto cupcakes. Sprinkle with remaining poppy seeds. Garnish with Candied Lemon Slices, if desired.

CANDIED LEMON SLICES:

Heat oven to 350°F. Bring ¼ cup each water and sugar to boil in small saucepan; cook 3 min. Cut 2 lemons lengthwise in half. Cut each half crosswise into 8 slices; place in single layer on parchment-covered baking sheet. Pour sugar syrup over lemons. Bake 30 min.; cool. Refrigerate until ready to garnish cupcakes.

TIP:

Sifting the powdered sugar ensures that the prepared icing will be smooth.

INDEX

ACKNOWLEDGEMENTS

CONTRIBUTORS

Photography:
Con Poulos

Assisted By:
Christina Holmes and Joey Popovich

Food Stylist:
Susie Theodorou

Assisted By:
Vivian Lui and Rachel Fielder

Prop Stylist:
Johanna Lowe

KRAFT FOODS

Brand Team:
Karen Keller, Jorge de Castro,
Nina Barton

Marketing Team:
Jill Baskin, Howard Friedman

President Cheese & Dairy:
George Zoghbi

Kraft Kitchens:
Julie Gulik

MCGARRYBOWEN

Art Direction and Design:
Melissa Stolt, Aaron Pedersen,
Russell Eadie, Michael Straznickas

Writer:
Dave Reger

Print Production:
Kate Osborne, Erika Pflederer

Account Management:
Kristin Detroy, Nicole Marriott,
Sarah Lamberson, Robin Osborne

Art Production:
Susan Cartland

Copy Editor:
Elaine Cooper

SPECIAL THANKS

Tim Scott, Jennifer Fogle, Jamie Uhler,
Steve Reese, Steve Reese Jr.,
Francesco Catalano, Eugene Kravstov,
Richard Bode, Brad Connor, Robin Ross,
Lori Hartnett, Sarah Radeke, Toni Lange,
Kathy Harrison, Cheryl Chrysler,
Devanee Washington, Jeanne Conlon,
Dawn Silverstein